T0087248

RHYTHMIC COMPOSITIONS
ETUDES FOR PERFORMANCE AND SIGHT READING
SMARTMUSIC LEVELS 5 - 8

Written by
Kit Chatham, Steve Murphy, & Joe Testa

Dedicated with much love to
Sandy Feldstein
(1940 – 2007)

Special Thanks to: Rob Grad, Scotty Bahler, Troy Wollwage, John Wittmann, Prudence Elliott, Aaron Felske, Jim Petercsak, Rob Shanahan, and SmartMusic

Cover Artwork: Rob Grad - IdeasInc.biz
Book Design and Engraving: Kit Chatham

www.PrincipalPercussionSeries.com

TABLE OF CONTENTS:

INTERMEDIATE

RHYTHMIC COMPOSITIONS

[PREFACE]

Sandy Feldstein helped to mentor and cultivate the careers of so many in the music industry. His positive influence reached hundreds of people throughout his life; but, for the select few within his inner circle, he had a very profound and intimate impact. I thank God everyday for the blessing to have been able to learn from, interact with, and love him as teacher, friend, and musical father figure.

Similar to many percussion educational works, it is through him that the **Principal Percussion Series** was born. Originally a project he and I were to work on together, his untimely passing left it my hands to finish. Knowing the scope of the project, I brought in two of my friends whom I felt are not only fine musicians but are well-respected educators in their own fields: Kit Chatham and Steve Murphy. With Kit and Steve's help, I believe we accomplished the original directive as outlined by SmartMusic, all the while keeping a bit of Sandy's essence through each page.

Rhythmic Compositions consists of three books – each dedicated to various difficulty levels as defined by SmartMusic guidelines: Easy (Levels 1-4), Intermediate (Levels 5-8), and Advanced (Levels 9-10). For each of the ten levels, 30 etudes were written with the original intent to be sight-reading pieces. Though the etudes are perfect for sight-reading, they also stand up on their own and can be utilized as individual, musical performance pieces.

All of these etudes can also be found on SmartMusic. If you are not familiar with this program, we highly suggest you take a look into it at www.smartmusic.com. The educational advantages presented by SmartMusic are truly incredible, and we are honored to have our books as some of their first percussion pieces. As a bonus feature on SmartMusic, you can find the audio files of all these etudes performed by Kit himself.

If you are not familiar with Sandy Feldstein, other than what you have read in this Preface, I encourage you to research his legacy on the web. The more you dig, the more you will be amazed. For the rest of my life, I will be indebted to him. He gave me so many opportunities and always encouraged me to pursue what has made me so much of what I am today. He is missed beyond verbal expression but lives forever in the hearts and deeds of all those he touched in his much too short, yet beautiful, life.

It is in Sandy's memory that we, the authors, hope you find years of enjoyment in using these books for yourself and your students.

Sincerely,
Joe Testa

ABOUT THE AUTHORS:

Kit Chatham is an internationally recognized percussionist, performer, recording artist, arranger, and educator. Kit's experience in many forms of percussion, including drum set, world percussion, orchestral percussion, and marching percussion, makes him a highly sought after performer & clinician and allows him to create a sound that is uniquely his own.

Kit currently resides in Las Vegas, Nevada, where he is the percussionist for Cirque du Soleil's production, *Viva ELVIS*. Kit has enjoyed performing on stages around the world. Before joining *Viva ELVIS*, he was the original percussionist/drummer for Cirque du Soleil's touring show, *Corteo*, which travelled all over North America and Japan; was the featured percussionist for *CyberJam* performing in London's West End; and was the featured snare soloist/percussionist for the Tony and Emmy Award winning Broadway show, *BLAST!*.

Kit has arranged, composed, designed, and instructed for some of the Nation's top music ensembles. This list includes such groups as the Crossmen Drum & Bugle Corp, The University of Georgia, Terminus Percussion Theatre, Atlanta Quest, Odyssey Percussion Theater, and numerous scholastic groups throughout North America.

Kit received his Bachelor's Degree in Music Education from The University of Georgia where he studied with Dr. Thomas McCutchen and Dr. Arvin Scott. While attending, he instructed and arranged for the 2000 Sudler Trophy winning University of Georgia Redcoat Band, performed in numerous ensembles, and toured Europe performing at many prestigious jazz festivals.

Kit continues to give clinics and master classes on percussion around the world and is a proud endorser of Vic Firth Sticks & Mallets, Yamaha Drums & Percussion, Sabian Cymbals, Evans Drumheads, Alternate Mode, and fXpansion Music Software. See more about Kit at *www.KitChatham.com*.

Steve Murphy, for the past 18 years, has been the band director at Onteora Middle/High School in Boiceville, NY. Steve serves as percussion caption head for the Kingston High School Marching Band in Kingston, NY, as well as the director of the Onteora Jazz Ensemble, the Onteora Marching Band, and the Onteora Percussion Ensemble. Under his direction, the Onteora Middle School Band has received numerous Gold and Silver ratings at NYSSMA Major Ensemble festivals; and the Onteora Marching Band is a former Musical Arts Conference "Class II" Champion and has earned several 1st Place awards at the annual New York City St. Patrick's Day Parade.

Steve received his Bachelor's of Music Education and Master's in Percussion Performance from the Crane School of Music at SUNY Potsdam where he studied with James Petercsak. Steve is also a member of MENC, the New York State School Music Association, the Percussive Arts Society, and the Ulster County Music Educators Association.

Joe Testa is highly respected in the music industry and began his career after earning a Bachelor of Music from the Crane School of Music at SUNY Potsdam, New York. He first put his knowledge into action working for Warner Bros Publications in Miami, Florida, under the tutelage of his mentor Sandy Feldstein. During this time, Joe became an accomplished editor, author, businessman, and leader himself. He produced, coordinated and authored best-selling instructional media with high-profile artists including Russ Miller, Gavin Harrison, and Akira Jimbo and respected educators such as Steve Houghton. Additionally, Joe orchestrated the creation of numerous instructional music publications and videos.

Joe moved to California when he became international artist relations manager for Yamaha Corporation of America. He was an extremely successful corporate event producer of the annual Groove Night and Groove All Stars drum events, which included special appearances by Michael McDonald, Jackson Browne, and Ellis Hall and were held in the US, Mexico and Germany. He proudly found himself working alongside celebrated drummers such as Rick Marotta, Steve Jordan, Carter Beauford, Manu Katche, Keith Carlock, and his own drum hero, Steve Gadd.

As a freelance producer, editor, writer, and consultant for publishing and visual marketing projects, Joe was the director and producer of Memphis Drum Shop's *Cymbal Summit 2010 Weekend* and of Mapex's Falcon promotional *Let Your Feet Fly* video. One of his most rewarding roles was as writer and video producer of MakeMusic Inc.'s Rudimental Project, which was SmartMusic's debut of online percussion material—a treasured project given to him by Sandy. Other clients include Sabian, Dreamland Recording Studios, Carl Fischer Music, and Warner Bros Publications.

Currently, Joe can be found in Massachusetts as director of artist relations for Vic Firth Company. There, he oversees the talent of over 2900 artists, including Cindy Blackman, Matt Cameron, Abe Laboriel Jr., and Charlie Watts. Joe is actively preparing, monitoring, and developing global projects and promotions including signature product contracts, artist signings, video production, educational tours, recording, film, tours, performances, and endorsements.

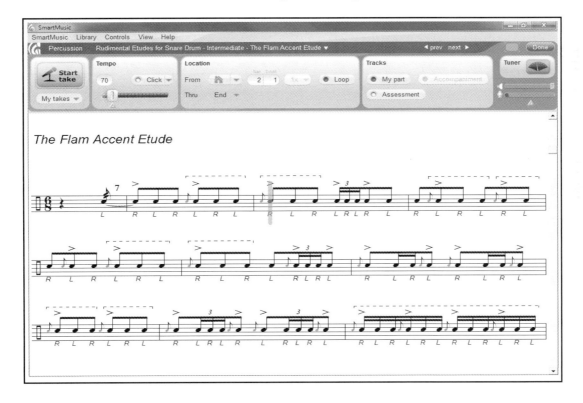

THE ROLL RUDIMENTS:

Rudiment is included in the Original 26

I. SINGLE STROKE ROLL RUDIMENTS

SINGLE STROKE ROLL*

R L R L R L R L

SINGLE STROKE 4

R L R L   L R L R

SINGLE STROKE 7

R L R L R L R
L R L R L R L

II. MULTIPLE BOUNCE ROLL RUDIMENTS

MULTIPLE BOUNCE ROLL

TRIPLE STROKE ROLL

R R R L L L R R R L L L

III. DOUBLE STROKE OPEN ROLL RUDIMENTS

DOUBLE STROKE OPEN ROLL*

RRLLRRLL

10 STROKE ROLL*

R   R L   R   R L
L   L R   L   L R

5 STROKE ROLL*

R   R   L   L

11 STROKE ROLL*

R   R L   R   R L
L   L R   L   L R

6 STROKE ROLL

R L   L R L   L

13 STROKE ROLL*

R   R L   R   L L

7 STROKE ROLL*

R   L   R   L

15 STROKE ROLL*

R   R   L R   R   L
L   R L   L R

9 STROKE ROLL*

R   R   L   L

17 STROKE ROLL

R   R
L   L

THE DIDDLE RUDIMENTS:

Rudiment is included in the Original 26

SINGLE PARADIDDLE*

R L R R L R L L

DOUBLE PARADIDDLE*

R L R L R R L R L R L L

TRIPLE PARADIDDLE

R L R L R L R R L R L R L R L L

SINGLE PARADIDDLE-DIDDLE

R L R R L L R L R R L L
L R L L R R L R L L R R

THE FLAM RUDIMENTS:

*Rudiment is included in the Original 26

FLAM*

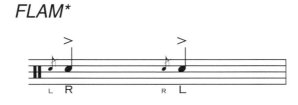

FLAM ACCENT*

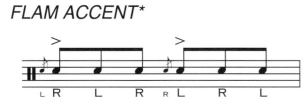

FLAM PARADIDDLE-DIDDLE*

FLAM TAP*

PATAFLAFLA

FLAMACUE*

SWISS ARMY TRIPLET

FLAM PARADIDDLE*

INVERTED FLAM TAP

SINGLE FLAMMED MILL

FLAM DRAG

THE DRAG RUDIMENTS:

Rudiment is included in the Original 26

DRAG *

DRAG PARADIDDLE #1 *

SINGLE DRAG TAP *

DRAG PARADIDDLE #2 *

DOUBLE DRAG TAP *

SINGLE RATAMACUE *

LESSON 25 *

DOUBLE RATAMACUE *

SINGLE DRAGADIDDLE

TRIPLE RATAMACUE *

SMARTMUSIC SIGHT READING ETUDE SPECIFICATIONS:

LEVEL 5 - *(in addition to levels 1 - 4 of the SmartMusic Sight Reading Level Specs)*

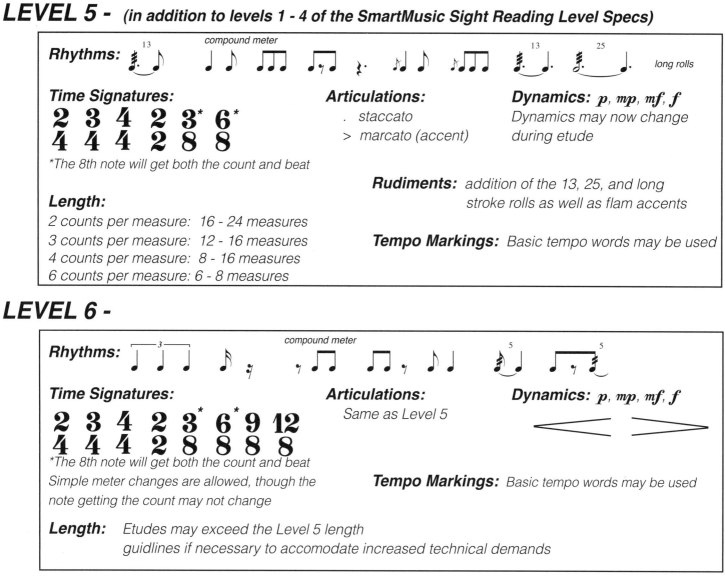

Rhythms: *compound meter* ... *long rolls*

Time Signatures:

$\frac{2}{4}$ $\frac{3}{4}$ $\frac{4}{4}$ $\frac{2}{2}$ $\frac{3^*}{8}$ $\frac{6^*}{8}$

*The 8th note will get both the count and beat

Length:
2 counts per measure: 16 - 24 measures
3 counts per measure: 12 - 16 measures
4 counts per measure: 8 - 16 measures
6 counts per measure: 6 - 8 measures

Articulations:
. staccato
> marcato (accent)

Dynamics: *p, mp, mf, f*
*Dynamics may now change
during etude*

Rudiments: addition of the 13, 25, and long
stroke rolls as well as flam accents

Tempo Markings: Basic tempo words may be used

LEVEL 6 -

Rhythms: *compound meter*

Time Signatures:

$\frac{2}{4}$ $\frac{3}{4}$ $\frac{4}{4}$ $\frac{2}{2}$ $\frac{3^*}{8}$ $\frac{6^*}{8}$ $\frac{9}{8}$ $\frac{12}{8}$

*The 8th note will get both the count and beat
*Simple meter changes are allowed, though the
note getting the count may not change*

Articulations:
Same as Level 5

Dynamics: *p, mp, mf, f*

Tempo Markings: Basic tempo words may be used

Length: Etudes may exceed the Level 5 length
guidlines if necessary to accomodate increased technical demands

LEVEL 7 -

Rhythms: *compound meter* ... *all rolls*

Time Signatures:
Same as level 6

Articulations:
Same as Level 5

Dynamics: *p, mp, mf, f*

Tempo Markings: Basic tempo words may be used

Length: - Each etude must form a musical whole and be long enough to asses the included
rhythmic, melodic, and musical concepts.
- Etudes should not be longer than 30 seconds.

LEVEL 8 -

Rhythms: *compound meter*

Time Signatures:
Same as level 6

Articulations:
Same as Level 5

Dynamics: *p, mp, mf, f*

Tempo Markings: Basic tempo words may be used

Length: Etudes should not be longer than 40 seconds.

RHYTHMIC COMPOSITIONS
LEVEL 5

Andante ♩. = 96 - 100

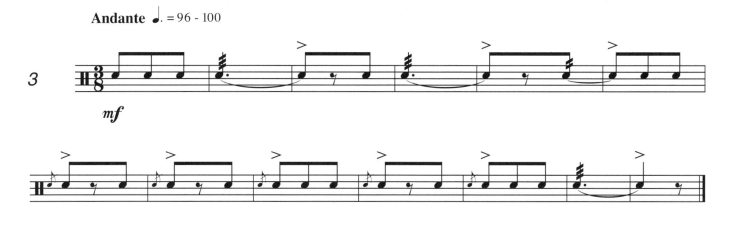

mf

Andante ♩. = 100 - 104

f

Moderato ♩ = 108 - 112

mf

p

f

p   *f*

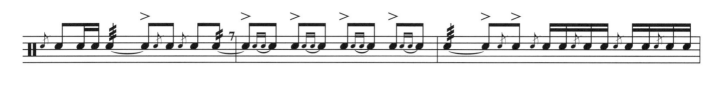

Andante ♩ = 88 - 92

Andante ♩ = 100 - 104

Andante ♩ = 104 - 108

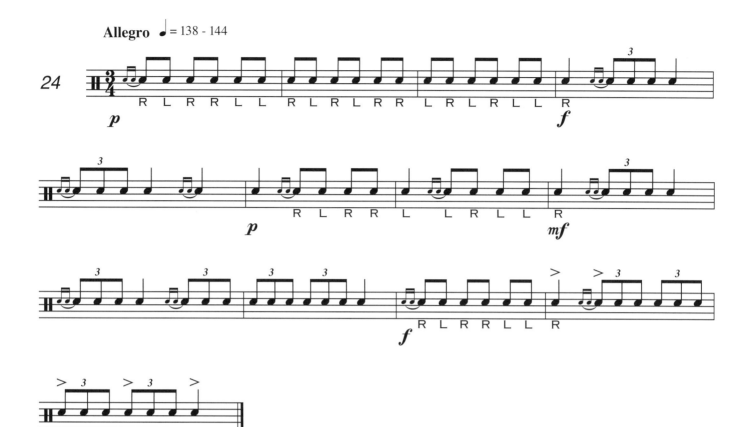

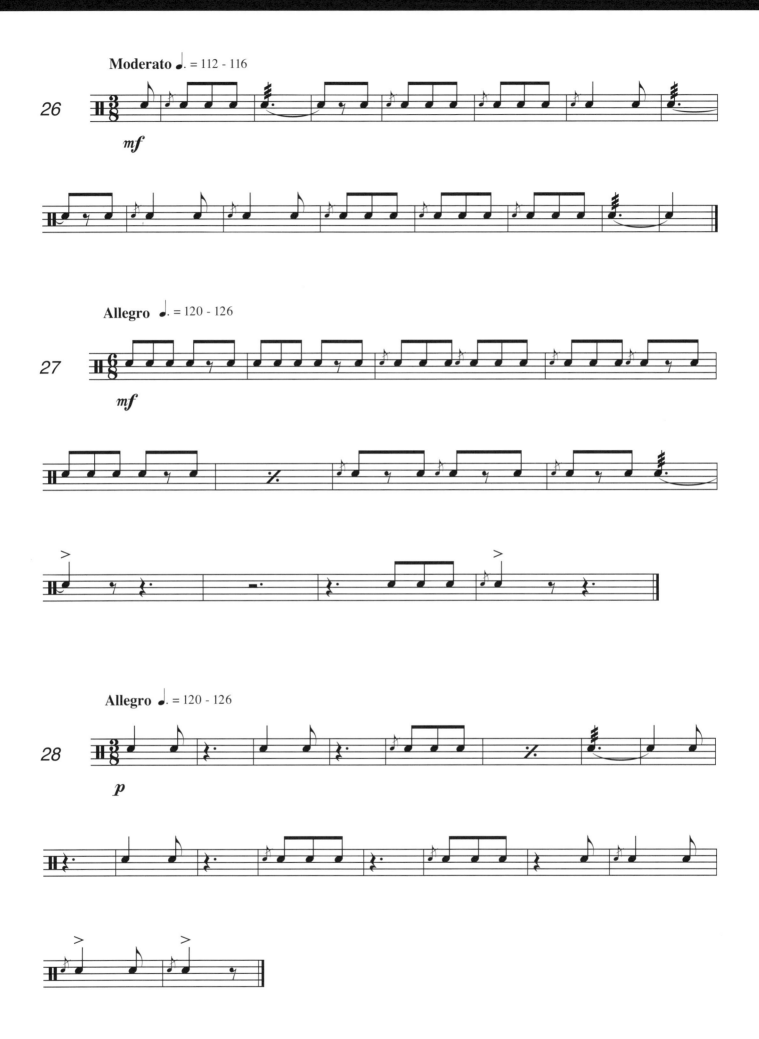

Allegro ♩. = 126 - 132

29

mf

Allegro ♩. = 132 - 138

30

mf

RHYTHMIC COMPOSITIONS
LEVEL 6

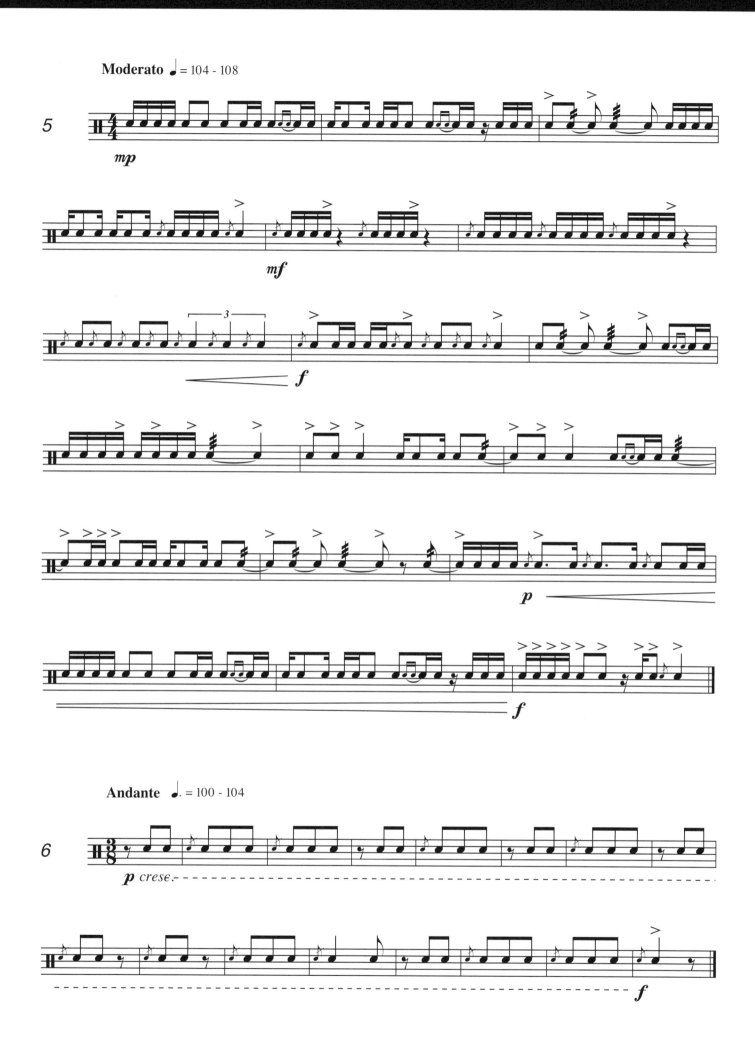

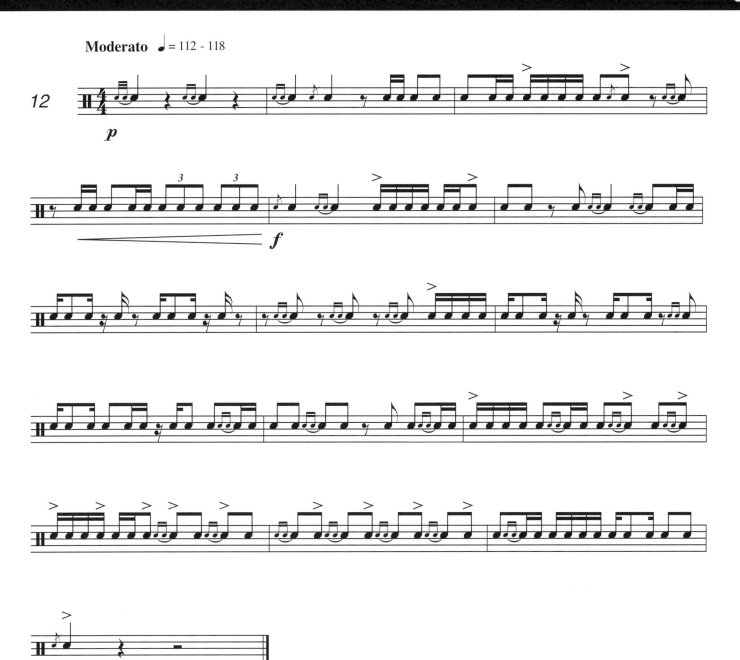

Moderato ♩ = 104 - 108

18

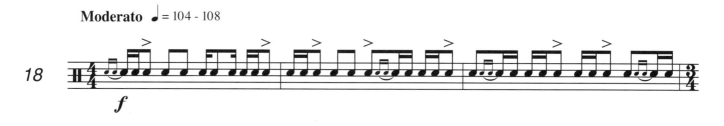

Moderato ♩. = 108 - 112

19

Moderato ♩. = 104 - 108

20

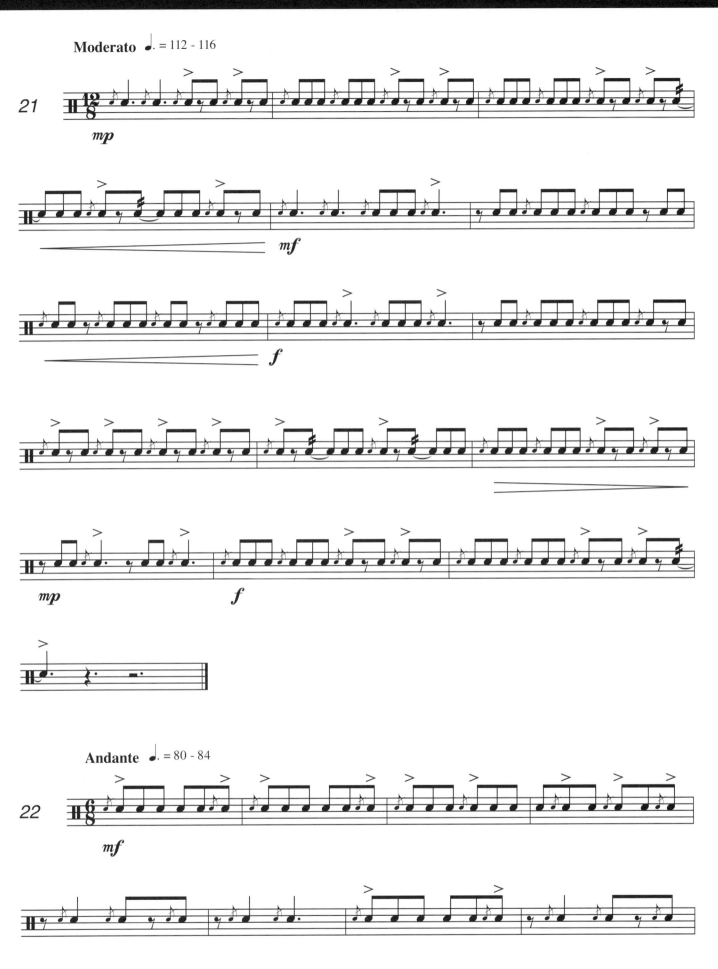

NOTES:

RHYTHMIC COMPOSITIONS
LEVEL 7

Moderato ♩ = 108 - 112

Andante ♩. = 84 - 88

Andante ♩ = 88 - 92

17

f

Andante ♩. = 72 - 76

18

f

mp

f

Andante ♩ = 88 - 92

21

f

Moderato ♩ = 112 - 118

22

f

Andante ♩. = 80 - 86

23

mf   *f*

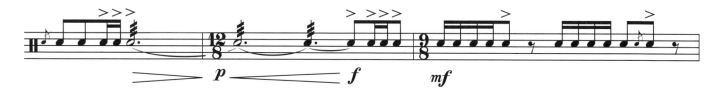

p   *f*   *mf*

f

p

Moderato ♩ = 110 - 116

24

mf

mp

mf

Andante ♩. = 82 - 90

28

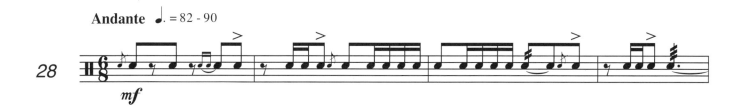

mf

p

mf

p

mf

f

p

f

p

f

RHYTHMIC COMPOSITIONS
LEVEL 8

Andante ♩. = 78 - 84

1

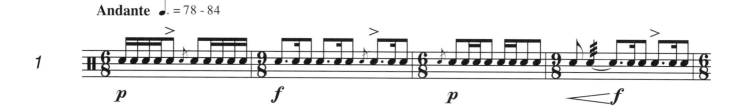

Andante ♩. = 86 - 92

2

Allegro ♩ = 122 - 128

Andante ♩. = 82 - 88

p

mf

mf

f   *p*

Andante ♩ = 86 - 94

6

mf

mp

f

mf

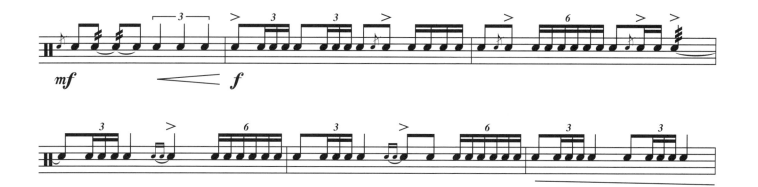

Andante ♩. = 88 - 96

9

Andante ♩ = 92 - 98

18

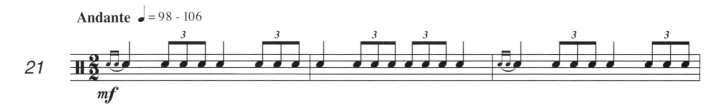

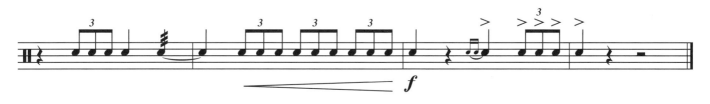

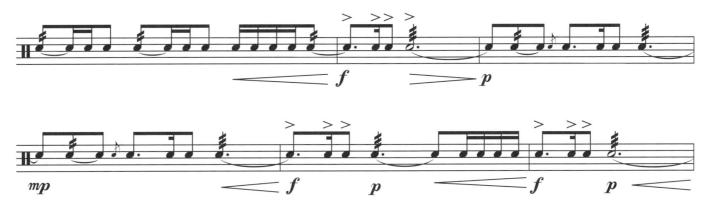

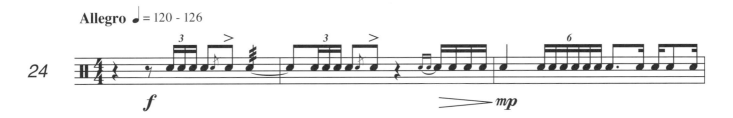

Andante ♩. = 78 - 84

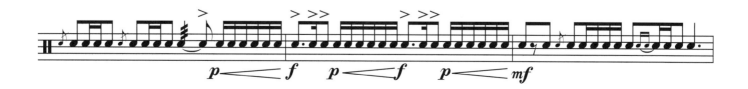

Allegro ♩ = 138 - 146

NOTES:

NOTES: